VICTORY IN CHRIST

THE GOD OF PEACE WILL CRUSH SATAN UNDER YOUR FEET.　ROMANS 16:20

TOM PATRICK

AVAILABLE FOR SALE at www.AMAZON.COM/BOOKS

WEEKLY BLOG FREE SUBSCRIPTION at www.TOMPATRICK.ORG

.

OTHER BOOKS BY TOM PATRICK

Christ for the Common Man   2023

.

.

.

ISBN – Paperback: 979-8-9874511-3-7

CONTENTS

PREFACE

Many Christians today totally miss the significance of the spirit world although God Himself is Spirit. We want to present ourselves as educated and sophisticated, not subject to superstitions or half-baked religion, so we end up limiting ourselves to the "real world" of the physical realm. Amazing! Claiming salvation by miraculous and supernatural means, we reject the other powers and aspects of the supernatural realm.

Unwilling to seriously study the demonic realm, we credit Satan and his followers with power that is totally unreal —-it's just not there. Satan is the impotent one —- but he's a fantastic liar and deceiver. And we deny ourselves the true authority Jesus promised to His followers while He was alive in the flesh and then He died to guarantee the promise. Remember this —- all the blessings and gifts of God come to us **by grace through faith**. The promises are merely offers until we believe and reach out to receive them. There is so much in the Bible that we are unwilling to believe and receive, and so we never experience it in our lives. We cheat ourselves.

Some chapters in this book are longer than others because some teaching points need more space to fully explain, and some require more scripture to verify God's truth. I am called to deepen our understanding of our God --- not to create great works of literature.

This is not a how-to-do-demons book. It is intended as a biblically sound, straightforward look at God and Satan as presented in the written Word of God. The church of today has over-rated the powers of Satan and under-rated, or sometimes totally missed, the authority that God offers to His followers in Christ.

I ask only two things :

1 that you read this book with an open mind, open to God.

2 that you read the Bible and believe it.

JESUS has a role in God's plan:

> **For this purpose the Son of God was manifested, that HE might destroy the works of the devil.   1 John 3:8**

YOU have a role in God's plan:

> **And the God of peace will crush Satan under YOUR feet.   Romans 16:20**

God bless us all,
Tom Patrick

CHAPTER 1

GOD GIVES DOMINION; MAN GIVES IT AWAY.

*Then God said, [to Himself as the Trinity] "Let Us make man in Our image, according to Our likeness; let them have dominion over the fish of the sea, over the birds of the air, and over the cattle, over all the earth and over every creeping thing that creeps on the earth." ²⁷ So God created man in His own image; in the image of God He created him; male and female He created them. ²⁸ Then God blessed them, and God said **to them**, "Be fruitful and multiply; fill the earth and subdue it; have **dominion** over the fish of the sea, over the birds of the air, and **over every living thing** that moves on the earth."*   *Genesis 1:26-28*

God is sovereign over all, with dominion over **all**,

that means everything, though we cannot possibly understand it. He creates the earth and mankind to inhabit it. Then He, meaning all three members of the Holy Trinity, conducts a meeting and He/They decide to give dominion over every living creature on earth to mankind. Then God creates mankind and gives to him that dominion, authority, sovereignty. With all this authority, God gives only one rule. You see that tree over there in the middle of the garden; you shall not eat the fruit from that one tree. *"The Lord God commanded the man, saying, "Of every tree of the garden you may freely eat; but of the tree of the knowledge of good and evil you shall not eat, for in the day that you eat of it you shall surely die."* Genesis 2:15-17 Life was good in the garden —- and fairly simple with only one rule to keep.

> *Now the serpent was more **cunning** than any beast of the field which the LORD God had made. And he said to the woman, "Has God indeed said, 'You shall not eat of every tree of the garden'?" Genesis 3:1*

I emphasize the word cunning, because that is the only weapon or power that Satan has! This Satan is the same archangel Lucifer who led a revolt in heaven to overthrow God. He lost; he and the angels who followed him were kicked out of heaven —- defeated and powerless. For His own reasons, God has allowed Satan to exist. You see, God created man to be His family. He created mankind in His own image whose very essence is love. **Love, to be genuine, requires free-**

dom —- the freedom to be given or be withheld. Love that is required or forced by design is slavery. Love that is bought or bribed is prostitution. And remember, mankind was created in the **image of God**, and God is totally **free.**

And so we find mankind is given total authority over the earth —- with only one rule to keep —- and total freedom to give or withhold his love and his obedience even to the God of all creation.

> *Now the serpent was more **cunning** than any beast of the field which the LORD God had made. And he said to the woman, "Has God indeed said, 'You shall not eat of every tree of the garden'?"*

Note how the cunning deceiver sounds so reasonable. beginning with a simple question. Did God really say that? And note how he quotes God perfectly except for a slight twist; "you shall NOT eat of every tree." "You will surely not die." Come on now; be reasonable. And then the final lie to clinch the deal; "You will be like God." Who can resist a pitch like that? It sounds so reasonable, and it's almost an exact quoting of God,

> *And the woman said to the serpent, "We may eat the fruit of the trees of the garden; ³ but of the fruit of the tree which is in the midst of the garden, God has said, 'You shall not eat it, nor shall you touch it, lest you die.'" ⁴ Then the serpent said to the woman, "You will not surely die. ⁵ For God knows that in the day you eat of it your eyes will be opened, and you will be like God, knowing good and evil." ⁶ So*

when the woman saw that the tree was good for food, that it was pleasant to the eyes, and a tree desirable to make one wise, she took of its fruit and ate. She also gave to her husband with her, and he ate. Genesis 3:2-6

Let's look at what went right and what went wrong.
Eve still caught his misquote; then she quoted God correctly. But the tree looked so good and the fruit so tempting —- and you will end up being like God —- who can resist that? I'll take it. And she took a bite and handed it to Adam. Men —- yea and hooray! We can blame all the world's problems on the woman. WRONG. Eve did not even exist when God gave those instructions to Adam. To his credit, he obviously had conveyed them correctly to Eve, but where was Adam when Satan was tempting his wife? Scripture doesn't tell us.

WHAT IF?
What if Adam had been there and firmly stepped in front of Eve and clearly said to the devil, "You're a scam, and you'd better get the hell away from my wife and never come back!" That's not very nice talk in this Christian book, but that would have changed the entire history of the world. Wouldn't it??? And what did Adam say later on when he saw God? "*Then the man (Adam) said, "**The woman** whom **You gave** to be with me, **she gave** me of the tree, and I ate."* Genesis 3:12 Adam said it's all that woman's fault —- and don't forget, "You gave her to me." What a man —- what a sorry excuse for a man. He is known as the first Adam, and Jesus is known as the second Adam. Men, which Adam will you use as the model for your life? We don't have time to go into a

study of manhood and womanhood —- but this would be the right place to start.

Back to our overview:

God created the earth —- created mankind —- gave to him dominion-sovereignty-authority over all the earth.

Mankind gave it away. He gave dominion-sovereignty-authority to Satan by yielding to his leading and lies. Pause to think about that.

When He walked the earth as man, Jesus referred to Satan three times as the **ruler of this world.** John 12:31; 14:30; 16:11

Paul called Satan the **god of this age.** 2 Corinthians 4:4

John's Revelation says *"Satan, who deceives the whole world ... was cast to the earth, and his angels were cast out with him."* Revelation 12:9

And so the world stage is set, and the spiritual warfare has begun. It's a battle for control, dominion, over the earth. And it is now being fought on earth between mankind and the forces of Satan.

YOU are involved because you are part of mankind. And if you are GOD's man or woman, you're really involved because Satan hates you fiercely.

For discussion and meditation:

Why did God give man dominion? Why not just let him hang out here with no responsibility? Is that related to being created in the **image of God?**

Genuine love requires freedom. Really? Let's think about that. We're back to that **image of God** because He is totally free.

Think about the man and woman and their response to Satan when he appeared —- and then to God when He appeared that evening.

How could Jesus call Satan "ruler of this world?" Remember, He said that before He was crucified.

This battle between God and Satan was fought in heaven, and God won. The same battle between God and Satan is being fought on earth today; who is doing the fighting? Who *appears* to be winning today?

CHAPTER 2

JESUS TAKES IT BACK AND OFFERS IT TO US.

Now you get the big picture. Satan came and deceived Adam and Eve into believing him and following his lead. God's purity and His law say the penalty for sin is death. Because Man committed that original sin, only a Man's death could fulfill God's law. And the death, or sacrifice, had to be a spotless or sinless, perfect Man. There was none. So God became a Man and came to earth to pay the price --- God sent His Son. Likewise, it was Man who gave away the **dominion-authority-sovereignty** over the earth to Satan. And only a Man could take it back --- redeem it. Adam and Eve gave it away; Jesus came to take it back.

In the garden that day:

1.   Man lost his **relationship** with God --- kicked out of the garden.

2.   Man corrupted the **image** of God in which he had been created.

3.   Man gave, or traded away his God-given **DOMIN-ION-AUTHORITY-SOVEREIGNTY** over the earth.

Only a man --- a perfect man --- could restore all that was lost that day. So God became a man and came here in person --- Jesus. By His death on the cross, our Lord bought back all that mankind had traded away. Jesus redeemed it and now gives it (OFFERS it) back to mankind. Remember that every gift of God and Christ begins as an OFFER --- and never goes beyond that until man agrees to receive it. Many want salvation, a restored **relationship** --- the fire insurance from hell. Some want a restored **image**; scripture calls it healing. Few want or understand God's restoration of **dominion** over the earth.

Hear Christ's last words as a living man, spoken just before death. *After this, Jesus, knowing that all things were now accomplished ... ... said, "It is finished!" And bowing His head, He gave up His spirit.*   John 19:28-30

"It is finished" As fully MAN, Jesus was saying, "*MY work as a man is finished. My work as the MAN, redeemer, sacrifice, and CONQUEROR of SATAN is finished. Now, it's your job.*" No, He didn't really say those words, but that's exactly how it is. Remember, His mission statement is clearly given in LUKE 4:18-19 and is taught for the remaining three years as what is called our Great Commission. Jesus then hands it off to us as our co-mission. We are the living Body of Christ on earth today. Now, it's our turn.

And Jesus came and spoke to them, saying, "All **authority** has been given to Me in heaven and on earth. [19] **Go** therefore and make disciples of all the nations, baptizing them in the

name of the Father and of the Son and of the
Holy Spirit, teaching them to observe [to **do**]
all things that I have commanded you; and lo,
I am with you always, even to the end of the
age." Matthew 28:18-20

He is saying "I give earthly authority, dominion back
to you. Now exercise it --- establish it. Get on with the
initial commands God gave to mankind; be fruitful and
multiply; subdue the earth." In other words, have a great
life, and I will always be with you. He is offering to put
things back like they were meant to be in the garden.
But Man must accept his responsibility and use his
God-given (offered) authority. Man must **accept** God's
authority and **use** it —- **do** the work as God's stewards
of the earth.

We cannot do it sitting safely in the church in our
prayer meetings. That's the perfect place for preparation, but we have to go out into the world to apply
the truth and will of God. We are the ones to make it
happen —- *"Thy will be done on earth as it is in heaven."*
**"My work is finished —- now it's your job as the Body
of Christ."** *(Patrick Paraphrase)*

*And the Word became flesh and dwelt among
us, and we beheld His glory, the glory as of the
only begotten of the Father, full of grace and
truth. John 1:14*

Dear Friends, it is God's will that His Word shall **continue** to become flesh —- **in your flesh** so the unsaved
world will continue to behold the glory, grace, and truth

of God as demonstrated **in your life**.

For discussion and meditation:

We can understand why God would want to restore the relationship with man and His image within man, but why does God care about restoring dominion-authority-sovereignty to man?

Jesus has completed His work as a human on earth. "It is finished." Why do we have to be involved now, and what is our work or responsibility?

Jesus was "the Word become flesh." Does God really want the Word, the essence of God, to become flesh **in my flesh** today? What does that mean? What would that look like?

How do we tie together the word becoming flesh idea with "created in the image of God?"

CHAPTER 3

SATAN HAS NO POWER AND NO AUTHORITY.

We find an introduction to Satan, originally the archangel, Lucifer, in Ezekiel 28:1-19. Lucifer was one of the highest-ranking angels in all of heaven, and he was truly magnificent. This is one of those scripture sections which speak on two levels; it speaks of Lucifer in heaven at the time and also speaks of the King of Tyre on earth. This is a long passage but well worth our time in reading.

> [1] The word of the Lord came to me again, saying, [2] "Son of man, say to the prince of Tyre, 'Thus says the Lord God:
> "Because your heart is lifted up,
> And you say, 'I am a god,
> I sit in the seat of gods,
> In the midst of the seas,'
> Yet you are a man, and not a god,
> Though you set your heart as the heart of a

god
vs[11] Moreover the word of the Lord came to
me, saying, [12] "Son of man, take up a lamen-
tation for the king of Tyre, and say to him,
'Thus says the Lord God:
"You were the seal of perfection,
Full of wisdom and perfect in beauty.
[13] You were in Eden, the garden of God;
Every precious stone was your covering:
The sardius, topaz, and diamond,
Beryl, onyx, and jasper,
Sapphire, turquoise, and emerald with gold.
The workmanship of your timbrels and
pipes [your voice]
Was prepared for you on the day you were
created.
[14] "You were the anointed cherub who covers;
I established you;
You were on the holy mountain of God;
You walked back and forth in the midst of
fiery stones.
[15] You were perfect in your ways from the day
you were created,
Till iniquity was found in you.
[16] "By the abundance of your trading
You became filled with violence within,
And you sinned;
Therefore I cast you as a profane thing
Out of the mountain of God;
And I destroyed you, O covering cherub,
From the midst of the fiery stones.
[17] "Your heart was lifted up because of your
beauty;

You corrupted your wisdom for the sake of
your splendor;
I cast you to the ground,
I laid you before kings,
That they might gaze at you.
¹⁸ "You defiled your sanctuaries
By the multitude of your iniquities,
By the iniquity of your trading;
Therefore I brought fire from your midst;
It devoured you,
And I turned you to ashes upon the earth
In the sight of all who saw you.
¹⁹ All who knew you among the peoples are
astonished at you;
You have become a horror,
And shall be no more forever.""""
Ezekiel 28:1-20

At the very beginning, we see the original sin revealed
in Lucifer —- **pride**. It's the same original sin revealed
in Adam and Eve in the garden on earth. *"Because your
heart is lifted up and you say, **'I am a god, I sit in the seat
of gods ...'"** verse 1. "Because you have set your heart as the
heart of a god..." verse 6 "You were in Eden, the garden of
God; every precious stone was your covering ... ." verse 19
You were the anointed cherub who covers..." verse 14* He
was one of the chosen warrior angels who hovered over
the throne. *"Your heart was lifted up because of your beauty.
You corrupted your wisdom for the sake of your splendor; ..."
verse 17* Do you get the picture of this exceptional,
beautiful, wise, high-ranking angel who gets caught up
in the original sin of the original competition to be
Almighty God —- the original false god of **SELF**. And

the original sin is clearly **PRIDE**.

We see further into the heart of this archangel in Isaiah 14. His sin is clearly and repeatedly identified as five times he proudly declares "**I will.**" He keeps building up himself until he finally believes **he will be like God**. Isn't that what he used to tempt Adam and Eve? The serpent said: *"For God knows that in the day you eat of it your eyes will be opened, and **you will be like God**, knowing good and evil." Genesis 3:5*

> *"How you are fallen from heaven, O Lucifer, son of the morning! How you are cut down to the ground, You who weakened the nations!* [13] *For you have said in your heart:* **I will** *ascend into heaven,* **I will** *exalt my throne above the stars of God;* **I will** *also sit on the mount of the congregation On the farthest sides of the north;* [14] **I will** *ascend above the heights of the clouds,* **I will be like the Most High**.' [15] *Yet you shall be brought down to Sheol, To the lowest depths of the Pit. Isaiah 14:12-15*

Jesus said *"I saw Satan fall like lightning from heaven."* Luke 10:18-19 And John's vision in Revelation describes the heavenly battle between God and Lucifer.

> *And war broke out in heaven: Michael and his angels fought with the dragon; and the dragon and his angels fought,* [8] *but they did not prevail, nor was a place found for them in heaven any longer. So the great dragon was cast out, that serpent of old, called the Devil and Satan, who **deceives** the whole world; he was cast to the earth, and his*

angels were cast out with him.   Revelation 12:7-9

Lucifer, now known as Satan, is called the great deceiver because that is the only power-authority-weapon he has —- only the great lie. It's the same lie that caused his own downfall —- **"I will be like the Most High."** It's the same old sin —- **pride.** It's the same old false god —- **SELF.** Satan peddles it to us today, and we too often buy into it.

I could go on and on, but you really should pause here and just meditate on this. Read it over and over. Say it in your own words over and over until you fully understand it down in your soul.

The spiritual war is still raging, no matter how you visualize it. Jesus has won His battle against this enemy. **"It is finished." Now He offers His victory to you** —- if you are willing to receive it. But along with His victory comes His mission —- **our co-mission** —- **"Thy kingdom come."** We are to be the Body of Christ carrying out His mission on earth today. Are you willing to accept that mission and enter the battle?

THE BOTTOM LINE:
Satan offers his sin and his false god of self. You be your own god.

Jesus offers His Salvation and the One true God. You live under His lordship.

Remember —- it is God's offer or the devil's offer —- **which will you choose?**

Satan's word is a lie and his power is a fraud.

Whom will you BELIEVE? FOLLOW? CHOOSE?

For discussion and meditation:

The original sin is **pride**, and the ultimate pride is "I will be **like God**."

The ultimate sin in our lives is exactly the same as Satan's sin: "I will **BE God**."

I will have dominion and total authority over my life. **I will make my own choices and be my own god.**

Isn't this what we really see all around us today? Give some examples.

Do I see some examples in my own life? Ouch! Give some examples.

CHAPTER 4

"GOD IS IN CONTROL"

"*God is in control.*" When life looks bleak, Christians love to hang their heads and murmur "Yes, but God is in control." The words are true --- but the theology flowing from there is so often false.

Yes, God **is** in control —- but He is **not** a controller.

Why did God allow that ...? How can a loving God let this happen? A friend with a cancer diagnosis once said "I'll never understand why God put this in my life." He is a wonderful and sincere Christian. How can bad things happen to good people when God is in control? That is taking a much too narrow view of the world and life. Again, the words are true, but the theology or life outlook flowing from that is not in line with the Bible. God created the world and gave laws or rules to go with it. He is a God of integrity and will not ordinarily violate His own rules. It's a fallen world because of man's original sin. God's nature is love and His gifts are loving.

The Integrity of God :

"I am the Lord God; I do not change." Malachi 3:6

God gave dominion-sovereignty-authority over all the earth to Mankind. He said, "YOU be in control."

> Then God blessed them, and God said to them, "Be fruitful and multiply; **fill the earth and subdue it; HAVE DOMINION** over the fish of the sea, over the birds of the air, and over every living thing that moves on the earth." Genesis 1:28

Mankind gave it away. He gave it to Satan by yielding to his leading and believing his lies.

> Then the serpent said to the woman, "You will not surely die. [5] For God knows that in the day you eat of it your eyes will be opened, and you will be like God, knowing good and evil." [6] So when the woman saw that the tree was good for food, that it was pleasant to the eyes, and a tree desirable to make one wise, she took of its fruit and ate. She also gave to her husband with her, and he ate. Genesis 3:4-6

Jesus bought it back. He redeemed it with His own lifeblood —- and now offers it back to Mankind as part

of salvation.

> To Him who loved us and washed us from
> our sins in His own blood, [6] and has made
> us kings and priests to His God and Father,
> to Him be glory and **dominion** forever and
> ever. Amen   Revelation 1:5-6

Our authority, rule, or kingship is from our position
in Christ. It is not our own authority, but Christ's authority granted to us so we might **be** the body of Christ
made manifest on earth. Everything Jesus offers to us
as Christians is so we may fulfill the will of the Father
and **be** witnesses to the world. We are His stewards.
Our dominion and authority come from Christ and our
position as "new creatures **in Christ.**"

> "But you shall receive power when the Holy
> Spirit has come upon you; and you shall **be**
> witnesses to Me in Jerusalem, and in all Judea
> and Samaria, and to the end of the earth." Acts
> 1:8

If mankind refuses to obey the laws of God or refuses
to receive and exercise the authority God and Christ
have **offered**, God will not step in and clean up the mess
that results. Our Heavenly Father is not a helicopter
parent. So yes, bad things do happen to good people.
It's part of this fallen world. Sometimes we can identify
the sin, mistake, or failure that caused it all, and sometimes we simply cannot. But God does not put diseases
and disasters onto His children in order to let us suffer

awhile. That would be totally contrary to all that God has revealed to us about Himself. Jesus clearly tells us "you will have troubles in the world, but be of good cheer for I have overcome the world." He promises us His ultimate victory —- but it is not to be a smooth and easy journey. It was not easy for Jesus and will not be for us —- the Bible says so. Through it all, He promises "I will never leave you nor forsake you."

This Fallen World:

> *Jesus said: "And from the days of John the Baptist until now **the kingdom** of heaven **suffers vio-lence**, and the violent **take it by force**." Matthew 11:12*

"**Violence**" = Greek BIAZZO = to be seized, taken by force, by violence. "**Force**" = Greek HARPAZO = to seize, carry off by force, **claim for one's self**, to snatch.
   The Kingdom of Heaven is intended for us now! *"Our Father who art in heaven, Thy kingdom come —- **this day** our **daily** bread ... ."* And yet it suffers; it is surrounded by, force and violence. There is a violent enemy, and you know his name.

> *So Jesus said to them again, "PEACE to you! As the Father has sent Me, I also send you. And when He had said this, He breathed on them, and said to them, "**Receive** the Holy Spirit." John 20:21-22*

Receive = Greek LAMBANO = **seize, lay hold.** It is an

active and very **aggressive** verb.

Why does this Prince of Peace talk so rough, speaking of violence in the world He created? It is because there is a violent and evil enemy out there hunting you to devour or destroy you. 1st Peter 5:8 If you want to understand His words, "Receive the Holy Spirit," just picture an NFL wide-receiver running downfield and knowing the pass is coming to him and half the opposing defense is coming after him to put him down. Now, you've got the picture. The NFL is no place for wimps. The Body of Christ is no place for wimps either.

Christianity is not for wimps; there is an enemy, and we must be willing to stand up to him in claiming the blessings of this new life to which Jesus is calling us. The great news is "Yes, God **is** in control." The challenging news is that we must be willing to reach and fight to receive His countless blessings. There is an enemy, and the Kingdom of God does suffer violence from his constant attacks. We are promised victory, Christ's victory, when we join Him in this warfare.

Jesus has already won the victory; now our task is to install it as reality here and now in our daily existence.

The Warfare:

Paul gives a vivid picture of spiritual warfare in Ephesians 6. Notice He tells us four times to **stand**. We are not to cower and hide nor run, but **stand** against the enemy who attacks the Kingdom of Heaven and those who live in it —- here and now, today. The enemy is not human, flesh and blood. The enemy is spiritual, demons and Satan himself. This is rough talk for a rough life of discipleship in a rough world. And we are to live **boldly**. Following Christ Jesus is not a calling to a soft life.

CONCLUSIONS:

God says YOU have dominion-sovereignty-authority. YOU are responsible for your life!

What do YOU want, and are YOU willing to fight for it? To seize it? To take it by force?

God will not fail to do His part --- we often fail do our part. And then we blame God and say HE is responsible. "God is in control. It was the will of God." We try to dodge our responsibility like Adam in the garden, "It was the woman, the woman YOU gave me." We live in a fallen world; somebody or something went wrong. And often we are the ones who went wrong. I cannot blame my stupid mistakes and sinful choices on God.

It's time for Christians to STAND and MAN UP —- if you want it.

For discussion and meditation:

God really is in ultimate control. So how can we fall into error, bad theology, with that?

Why do we love to avoid responsibility and even hold someone else responsible for our decisions?

I have a job and a place in the community, proclaiming Jesus could cost me. What should I do?

Really? And why? Do you really beileve this?

I thought Christianity was for nice people; how can this talk of violence be true?

CHAPTER 5

UNDERSTANDING THE ENEMY

P aul gives a vivid picture of spiritual warfare in Ephesians 6. Notice He tells us four times to **stand**. We are not to cower and hide nor run, but **stand** against the enemy who attacks the Kingdom of Heaven and those who live in it —- here and now, today. The enemy is not human, flesh and blood. The enemy is spiritual, demons and Satan himself. This is rough talk for a rough life of discipleship in a rough world. And we are to live **boldly**. Following Christ Jesus is not a calling to a soft life.

> Finally, my brethren, be strong in the Lord and in the power of His might. [11] Put on the whole armor *of God, that you may be able to* **stand** *against the wiles of the devil.* [12] *For we do not wrestle against flesh and blood, but against principalities, against powers, against the rulers of the darkness of this age, against spiritual hosts* **[armies]** *of wickedness in the heavenly places.* [13] *Therefore take up the whole armor of God, that*

*you may be able to **withstand** in the evil day, and having done all, to **stand**. [14] **Stand** therefore, having girded your waist with truth, having put on the breastplate of righteousness, [15] and having shod your feet with the preparation of the gospel of peace; [16] above all, taking the shield of faith with which you will be able to quench all the fiery darts of the wicked one. [17] And take the helmet of salvation, and the sword of the Spirit, which is the word of God; [18] praying always with all prayer and supplication in the Spirit, being watchful to this end with all perseverance and supplication for all the saints— [19] and for me, that utterance may be given to me, that I may open my mouth **boldly** to make known the mystery of the gospel, [20] for which I am an ambassador in chains; that in it I may speak **boldly**, as I ought to speak.   Ephesians 6:10-20*

THE ENEMY —- let's break it down.

"We do not wrestle against flesh and blood, but against principalities, against powers, against the rulers of the darkness of this age, against spiritual hosts [**armies**] of wickedness in the heavenly places." Paul is telling us the enemy is spiritual, not human. We are talking about the unseen spiritual realm and the "heavenly places" which lie between our place in earth and God's throne in heaven. In 2nd Corinthians 12:2-3, Paul speaks of a man who was "caught up into the third heaven" which he also calls "paradise." Assuming that God can count to three, that tells me there is also a first and second heaven with the visible sun-moon-stars being the first heaven and all of whatever lies in between being the second heaven. Satan and his demons are all fallen angels; they can and do operate in that unseen spirit realm as well as in our visible physical realm here on earth.

When Daniel was in distress, he prayed to God and God sent an angel. Here is the story.

> Suddenly, a hand touched me, which made me tremble on my knees and on the palms of my hands. [11] And he [the angel] said to me, "O Daniel, man greatly beloved, understand the words that I speak to you, and stand upright, for I have now been sent to you." While he was speaking this word to me, I stood trembling. [12] Then he said to me, "Do not fear, Daniel, for **from the first day** that you set your heart to understand, and to humble yourself before your God, **your words were heard**; and I have come because of your words. [13] But the **prince of the kingdom of Persia withstood me twenty-one days**; and behold, **Michael**, one of the **chief princes**, came to help me, for I had been left alone there with the **kings of Persia.** [14] Now I have come to make you understand what will happen to your people in the latter days, for the vision refers to many days yet to come." Daniel 10:10-14

The angel says God heard Daniel's prayer and dispatched this angel immediately, but he was delayed

twenty-one days by a demon whom he identifies as
"prince of the kingdom of Persia." This angel had to
call on Michael for help in the fight. Michael is the
archangel in command of God's warrior angels; the
angel calls him "one of the **chief princes**." For some
reason in this telling, a prince seems to outrank or be
above a king as he refers to "the kings of Persia." So
one demonic prince and multiple kings were assigned
to Persia by Satan. Before leaving, this angel speaks of
princes and kings of Babylon. Greece, and Rome; all
of these are empires that battled against Israel. And
clearly, the demons (princes and kings) are assigned to
certain geographic territories. We don't think of that,
but there is organization among Satan's realm of ser-
vants just as there is among God's. Remember, Satan
and his group were once in heaven as God's angels.

> Then he said, "Do you know why I have come
> to you? And now I must return to fight with
> the **prince of Persia**; and when I have gone
> forth, indeed the **prince of Greece** will come.
> [21] But I will tell you what is noted in the Scrip-
> ture of Truth. No one upholds me against
> these, except Michael **your prince**.   Daniel
> 10:20-21

The angel says that when he leaves he will have to
fight the territorial demon **prince of Persia** again and
later the territorial demon **prince of Greece** will appear
and must be fought. Note that Israel was conquered by
Persia and later by Greece; so we see that demonic
territorial princes, assigned by Satan, are involved in

the fate of Israel.

The demons, fallen angels, are organized by rank or authority just as God's angels are. Likewise they can be **assigned to earthly territories**. The angel refers to Michael as **your prince** —- assigned to Isreal. In the Bible, when you see angelic activity connected with Israel, Michael is usually the angel involved. You might think of Michael as the archangel God has assigned to watch over Israel —- a "guardian angel." Here we see a guardian angel watching over God's people. Think about that.

How tough do you have to be?

Paul says **just try** —- just **resist** the devil.

> *Therefore **humble** [at PEACE] yourselves under the mighty hand of God, that He may exalt you in due time, ⁷ casting all your care upon Him, for He cares for you. ⁸ Be sober [calm, abstain from wine], be vigilant; because your adversary the devil walks about like a roaring lion, seeking whom he may devour. ⁹ **Resist** him, steadfast in the faith, knowing that the same sufferings are experienced by your brotherhood in the world. ¹⁰ But may the God of all grace, who called us to His eternal glory by Christ Jesus, after you have suffered a while, perfect, establish, strengthen, and settle you. 1 Peter 5:6-10*

Why does the devil roar, like a roaring lion? It's because that's all he has !!! It's because he has no power —-

no authority —- nothing but intimidation and bluff.

*"God resists the proud, But gives grace to the **humble**."* [7]
*Therefore submit to God. **Resist the devil and he will flee**
from you.* [8] *Draw near to God and He will draw near to you.*
James 4:-8

When you are proud — God resists you. Go back to
look at Lucifer in Isaiah and Ezekiel

**When you are humble and standing strong in your
faith —- God protects you.** *"Resist the devil, and he will
flee from you."*

CONCLUSIONS

God will not fail to do His part --- we fail do our part.

And then we blame God --- saying HE is responsible.
"God is in control. It was the will of God."

We try to dodge our responsibility just like Adam in
the garden, "it was the woman, the woman YOU gave
me."

"God is in control —- surely this must be His will."

Jesus said His kingdom suffers violence here on earth,
and if you want it here on earth, you have to "take it by
force."

It's time for Christians to STAND and MAN UP if you
really want the Kingdom of God right here and right
now..

For discussion and meditation:

Should I really believe all this about spiritual warfare in
the heavens between good and bad angels, or is this just

some fairy tale part of ancient history? Does this really go on today?

What does spiritual warfare look like in a person's life? Give an example?

Does it always have to be some huge thing happening in my life, or can Satan cause a lot of trouble with a constant stream of little things?

Jesus said "I will never leave you nor forsake you." So, that means He is always here to help me in the fight?

If God assigned the archangel Michael to watch over His people, could He possibly assign an angel to watch over me?

Scripture says if I just resist the devil he will flee. Could Satan be scared of the unseen angel who stands beside me???

CHAPTER 6

YOU ARE IN CONTROL.

---

*Therefore **humble** yourselves under the mighty hand of God, that He may exalt you in due time, ⁷ casting all your care upon Him, for He cares for you. ⁸ Be sober [calm, abstain from wine], be vigilant; because **your adversary** the devil walks about like a **roaring** lion, seeking whom he may **devour**. ⁹ **Resist** him, steadfast in the **faith**, knowing that the same sufferings are experienced by your brotherhood in the world.   1 Peter 5:6-9*

W hy does the devil roar, like a roaring lion? It's because that's all he has !!!

No power —- No authority —- Nothing but intimidation, bluff, lies, cunning.

Peter says just stay calm and walk humbly in God's care, knowing that God will take care of you in His own way and His own time. But always be vigilant because the Devil is always there, and he's always coming after you.

I don't care for the word devour, so I looked up the Greek —- it really is devour —- to eat or drink voraciously. And using it as a metaphor, I have seen it in operation in real life! Satan will eat a man alive. I have two friends of differing generations; one is deceased, but both were eaten alive by the same demon we refer to as alcoholism. Both grew up in the same church, and it's a strong church. Both prospered in the world with success, beautiful families, homes, and toys. The one now deceased had everything the world could provide —- but not the love, joy, peace, patience, and other fruit of a spiritually rich life. It was available to him; he was just not able to receive it through the alcohol. One day, at what should have been a healthy age, he went into the hospital and directly into intensive care as his organs began to shut down. One by one Satan would "devour" this good man, one organ at a time. He was a good man, a kind-hearted man, and my friend. But he had embraced the bottle as a way of life in college and just never could turn it loose —- despite all the treatments and care that money could buy. The devil devoured him. My other friend is a similar story of success and the good life —- but there is this bottle. At what should be a healthy age, he is unable or unwilling to care for himself and has physical issues —- because of the bottle. A toe had to be amputated, then others, then a foot, and so the story continues. Sin and Satan are never satisfied. Does he still have choices? Absolutely yes —- but there is this bottle. Do you see the picture, the metaphor of demons eating a man alive? And we're not talking about being saved or lost here; we're talking about the spiritual battle raging "in the heavenly places" and in the homes and hearts of men and women —-

both the saved and the lost —- every day. It is real!

I'll bet you missed it; not one in a hundred will see that.

There is a word that appears twice in the above scripture and which I deliberately did not print in bold —- "may." **"Can"** requires ability. **"May"** requires permission. It says "that He [God] **may exalt** you in due time," and the devil is "seeking whom he **may devour."**

Whose permission is required???? YOURS.

You have authority over your life. YOU CHOOSE !

God wants to exalt you; Satan wants to devour you.
YOU CHOOSE !

Both require your permission! YOU CHOOSE !

You have dominion-sovereignty-authority over your life. YOU CHOOSE !

You are responsible for your life! YOU CHOOSE !

What do you really want in life —- and are you willing to fight for it????

Let's take a break so you can meditate on this, and I'm getting tired from yelling at you.

How can you handle this devil who constantly is trying to destroy you?

> "God **resists** the proud, But gives grace to the humble." [7] Therefore submit to God. **Resist the devil** and **he will flee** from you. [8] Draw near to God and He will draw near to you. James 4:-8

There's that word humble again; Peter and James

both begin with humility before God. When you are proud, **God resists you** —- go back to look at the example of Lucifer in Isaiah and Ezekiel. When you are humble and standing strong in your faith —- **God protects you.** *"Resist the devil, and he will flee from you."* And Peter said **God will exalt you.**

Paul says put on the armor God gives and **stand, withstand, stand, stand.** James says **resist, and he will flee from you.**

Are you listening? We don't have to be some physical, mental, or even spiritual giant. We just have to try —- stand up and resist—- push back. Just try, and God will make up the difference. Holy Spirit always does the heavy lifting in the life of a spirit-filled believer.

You have dominion, sovereignty, and authority over your life.

You are responsible for your life.

What do you really want, and are you willing to fight for it?

I close with this same verse which is filled with God's truth. And note the last sentence; these same trials occur in every family —- **including our "Christian" homes.**

> *Therefore humble yourselves under the mighty hand of God, that He may exalt you in due time,* [7] *casting all your care upon Him, for He cares for you.* [8] *Be sober [calm, abstain from wine], be vigilant; because your adversary the devil walks about like a roaring lion, seeking whom he may devour.* [9] ***Resist*** *him, steadfast in the* ***faith***, *knowing that* ***the same sufferings are experienced by your brotherhood*** *in the world.   1 Peter 5:6-9*

For discussion and meditation:

All this suffering is going on with Christians, and the devil is trying to destroy us; should I trust the Bible in all this talk about sovereignty and God's authority being actually given to me?

Does this mean I can use God's authority and power to do anything I want?

The Bible says Satan **may** not destroy me without my permission; that's hard to believe. Let's talk about it.

The Bible says I must humble myself before God so He **may** exalt me? Why? That doesn't sound right, and how can humility be so important before God? It must have something to do with earlier chapters of this book where men did not humble themselves but sought to be equal to God. What happened to them? What happened to Lucifer?

It looks like God doesn't exactly give me a magic wand to control my life, but my choices do decide (control) much of what will happen in my life. What are some examples?

Maybe if I would study how God has set things up to work in the first place and just play by His rules, my life would go a lot better. Do you think so?

Maybe "God is in control" means in the beginning He set the world and all of life to operate a certain way —- **according to His rules** —- and now **I have a choice** to follow His rules or proudly fight against them and "be my own man."

Maybe I have a fresh choice and must choose every morning?

"Now therefore, fear the Lord, serve Him in sincerity and in truth, ... And if it seems wrong to you to serve the Lord, choose for yourselves this day whom you will serve, whether the gods which your fathers served that were on the other side of the River, or the gods of the [**Americans**] Amorites, in whose land you dwell. **But as for me and my house, we will serve the Lord.**"   Joshua 24:14-15

As for me, for this one day —- just one day —- whom will I serve????

CHAPTER 7

POSSESSED, OPPRESSED, OR DEPRESSED?

I ntellectuals and amateur theologians love to argue the finer points of the demonic. Scripture does speak of demonic possession and oppression.

The New Testament tells of numerous men who were demon-possessed. And it's true; a Christian can never be possessed by a demon. Paul assures us of that; Jesus paid a tremendous price for you.

> Or do you not know that your body is the temple of the Holy Spirit who is in you, whom you have from God, and **you are not your own?** [20] For **you were bought at a price**; therefore glorify God in your body and in your spirit, which are God's. 1 Corinthians 6:19-20

Scripture tells us of men who were **oppressed —-by the devil —-** and Jesus went about **healing all** of them. There are times when He is reported to heal all who were sick and times when only one or some were healed. But in Acts chapter 10, Luke states that Jesus healed **all** who were oppressed **by the devil.** This outright attack by the devil gets special attention unlike ordinary diseases and disorders "for God was with him." Satan is the direct enemy of God, and it seems God will not overlook when he attacks.

> God anointed Jesus of Nazareth with the Holy Spirit and with power, who went about doing good and **healing all who were oppressed by the devil, for God was with Him.**   Acts 10:38

Depression is mentioned in scripture but not as much as the other levels. But if you want to see a picture of ongoing depression, just look at King David and read the Psalms. David was known as a man after God's own heart, but he knew how he had often failed his God. And so David's own heart was often depressed —- "Why are you cast down, oh my soul?" Notice how many of the psalms begin in depression and sorrow as David is looking down in shame at his own sin and failure. But by the final verses, he has lifted his eyes and his focus to his God and what is written; and he closes the psalm rejoicing in hope again.

> Anxiety **in the heart of man** causes **depression,** but **a good word** makes it glad. Proverbs 12:25

Possessed, oppressed, or depressed —- the Bible

doesn't seem to differentiate.

Scripture seems to treat it all as demonic, coming from the devil, and something to be "healed" or "cast out" by the power of God. Remember, Lucifer/Satan led a revolution against God in heaven, and they are eternal enemies. Period !!! So if the Bible doesn't get into the differences, why should we? It's all of the devil and all to be defeated by the power of God. Today, the term **demonized** is often used to indicate the presence and influence of Satan or his demons. That is excellent wording; it presents the reality without making it something sensational.

Depression is so commonplace these days, it is often called "the common cold of mental health." And yes, **not** every depression involves the demonic. **Some do; some don't; all may**. I think of demons the same way I think of germs. The person who ignores the demonic is a fool just inviting trouble, and the one who is obsessed with it is sick and avoiding the truth. Some Christians seem to say "we don't do germs" as if they aren't allowed in our neighborhood. Oh, they're found in the projects and homeless camps downtown but not here; this is a nice neighborhood. You would never send your small child into the bathroom at McDonalds and say "Don't bother to wash your hands, this is a nice neighborhood." Jesus treats demons as ordinary, commonplace things to be dealt with each time they are encountered! They are always real, and they are always the enemy — God's, Christ's, and YOURS. We will come back to look at this in a later chapter.

For discussion and meditation:

If God doesn't make a big deal out of possessed or oppressed, why do we?

If Jesus treats the demonic as simply a part of the spirit realm that is constantly active in the physical realm, why don't we?

If scripture treats the demonic as ordinary and commonplace, why do we deny ever having experienced it? Are we somehow immune? Or are we simply blind?

Or is scripture wrong? After all, our denominational practices essentially ignore the subject.

Our creeds may mention it, but preaching and actual practices ignore it.

Does it really matter?

CHAPTER 8

AUTHORITY: JESUS SHOWS US HOW TO USE IT.

I love Jesus; He was an incredible man on earth —- always calm and cool under pressure. He never worried and never hurried; He simply walked into every situation confident of who He was in union with God the Father and God the Spirit. Scripture tells us He faced every temptation and emotion that we do; yet He never yielded to fear. **"We can handle this."** That's His example for us; that's just His way —- His truth —- His life.

> Then they went into Capernaum, and immediately on the Sabbath He entered **the synagogue** and **taught**. [22] And they were astonished at His teaching, for He taught them as one having **authority**, and not as the scribes. [23] Now there was a man in their synagogue with an unclean spirit. And he cried out, [24] saying, "Let **us** alone! What have we to do

with You, Jesus of Nazareth? Did You come to destroy us? **I know who You are—the Holy One of God!**"

25 But Jesus rebuked him, saying, "**Be quiet**, and **come out** of him!" 26 And when the unclean spirit had convulsed him and cried out with a loud voice, he came out of him. 27 Then they were all amazed, so that they questioned among themselves, saying, "What is this? What **new doctrine** is this? For **with authority He commands** even the unclean spirits, and they obey Him." Mark 1:21-27

Amazing! Jesus never ceases to fulfill, and man never ceases to disappoint and miss the point. This is on the Sabbath, and they are all in church. Jesus is teaching, and it's all wonderful —- the people are impressed with the sermon and amazed as He seems to have genuine authority. "Wow, I wonder where He went to seminary; this rabbi Jesus is really smart. He has great theology." The service was going great, and nobody knew the place was filled with demons as they filled this man. Nobody recognized problems in the man; he probably was dressed very nicely and fit right in. Nobody recognized Jesus either. "Who is this guy and how does he speak with such authority? Why do even the demons obey him? Who is this guy?"

But the demons recognized Jesus, and they feared Him. "Let us alone! What have we to do with You, Jesus of Nazareth? Did You come to destroy us? **I know who You are—the Holy One of God!**" Everyone else was just enjoying a nice routine church service; it's all good. But the demons knew exactly who He was.

How did Jesus handle it? Cool. He didn't ignore or try to avoid it; He simply confronted it. "**Be quiet**, and **come out** of him!" That's pretty simple and straightforward. Shut up and get out. Attention, you readers who are intellectuals, did Jesus debate or dialogue with the demon? Nope —- shut up and get out. It was never a matter of **knowledge or intelligence** —- it was **authority**. The amateur theologians present that day wanted to discuss "what new **doctrine** is this?" It was never about church doctrine —- it was about obedience —- to God's authority. Jesus later said, "All authority has been given to Me in heaven and on earth." Matthew 28:18

Jesus knew He had the God-given authority, and He exercised it. No big deal —- end of story.

Jesus wants us to be like that —- why do we resist believing that?

Dear friends, this is the model Jesus sets before you and me. When you know what the Savior offers to you and you fully accept it, then you can live in it. You can walk without fear knowing you're not alone and knowing the Son of God has given the authority of God into your hands. And you can exercise this God-given authority the same way Jesus did; you speak it —- the same way God did when He created the heavens and the earth; He spoke it. That's how God exercises His authority. That's how Jesus exercises His authority. That's how you and I are to exercise authority when the authority of God has been offered to us. And by the way, God always backs up His **authority** with His **power**.

You can do that. But first, you must be willing to **believe** it and **receive** it. Are you willing? Do you want it? Do you want the authority of God in your life —- or just some more church doctrine? We will look at this again in a later chapter.

I could go on and on looking at every time Jesus confronts demons in scripture, but the lesson is the same. The demon stories are fascinating and filled with lessons on practical Christian living in a fallen world. But Jesus is the same and His example for us remains the same. The powers of Satan were and still are at large in this world because the spiritual war, the battle between God and Satan, continues. The victory has been won —- at Calvary —- but the battle continues. And it will continue until one day, in God's timing, when Satan and his forces are thrown into the lake of fire forever. By the way, did you know that hell was not created for mankind? It was created for the devil and his followers, the demons, because they rejected God and rebelled against Him. When a man rejects Christ and follows the devil, that man will follow him all the way into hell and eternal damnation, just like the demons. In this life we make our choice whom we will follow —- and it will be eternal.

> "Then He will also say to those on the left hand, 'Depart from Me, you cursed, into the everlasting fire **prepared for the devil and his angels**: ... ... [46] And these will go away into everlasting punishment, but the righteous into eternal life." Matthew 25:41-46

It doesn't have to be that way. Jesus came to offer a choice. And with that choice, He offers us the same Holy Spirit anointing He had and the same authority. It is a valid offer —- do you want it?

For discussion and meditation:

How could a man be filled with demons and sit in a church service, yet nobody knows it?

Could that happen in your church today?

How could the demons be the only ones who understood the authority of Jesus?

How could Jesus be so calm when confronted by demons? Could you be that calm?

The people recognized Christ's authority but couldn't find it in their church doctrine. Is such authority part of your church's doctrine?

Is all this taught in your church and denomination?

CHAPTER 9

AUTHORITY: JESUS OFFERS IT TO YOU.

I n Luke chapter ten, the seventy have just returned from their mission trip; they can hardly believe what happened as they moved in Christ's authority, "in Your name." This is after the twelve disciples had been sent on a similar mission. This group of seventy did not include the disciples; these were just ordinary people who had been following Jesus and absorbing His teaching. They were more like you and me.

> Then the seventy returned with joy, saying, "Lord, even the demons are subject to us in Your name."
> [18] And He said to them, "I saw Satan fall like lightning from heaven. [19] **Behold, I give you the authority to trample on serpents and scorpions, and over all the power of the enemy,** and nothing shall by any means hurt you. Luke 10:17-19

Jesus makes a simple statement, what English teachers call a simple declaratory sentence: **"I give you authority."** There is a subject, verb, and direct object. It is unconditional; there is no if or when involved. The setting does indicate two requirements or conditions. **1.** He is speaking to His followers, **believers. 2.** They must be **willing to receive** what He wants to give.

If you can meet these two conditions, this offer is made to you.

Please note that all the gifts of God are merely offers —- until you are willing to receive them. **All of God's blessings are received "by grace through faith" —- ALL of them.** God's hand of grace reaches down from heaven to give you His unmerited gifts. Your hand of faith must reach up **and** be willing to receive what is in His hand. Faith is required because you can never see God's hand and what it holds for you. You must reach up into the unseen realm and be willing to receive whatever His hand holds. **That is faith.**

Do you understand this incredible gift/offer of God's authority? Jesus does not want you to do battle, actual combat, with the devil and his demons. Do you realize the power an angel can have? Let's look at what one angel can do, just one.

> And it came to pass on a certain night that the angel of the Lord went out, and killed in the camp of the Assyrians **one hundred and eighty-five thousand**; and when people arose early in the morning, there were the corpses—all dead. 2 Kings 19:35

That's just one angel in one night, and he's a good angel. Imagine what one rogue angel, a demon, could do —- or what several thousand in one person could do. Do you really want to fight with a guy like that??? Jesus wants you to do **spiritual** battle, not physical battle. He offers you **authority to command**, not power to physically engage. Let's dive deeper into this Word. In the Bible, the most often used word for power is the Greek "dunamis." We get our word dynamite from this. The word used here is authority; in Greek it's "exousia." But this "exousia" is also translated in the Bible as power. Authority conveys power. Without power flowing from the authority, it is meaningless. It is useless without the power needed to enforce it. Jesus is offering today His "exousia" authority —- **the full authority and power of God in heaven**. Do you qualify as a Christian? Do you want it?

It is to protect you and for you to use in fulfilling the Great Co-mission. In Luke 4:18, Jesus presents His personal mission statement; it comes to us from the Word of God, the pen of Isaiah, and the lips of Jesus. That's **VALID.** Jesus teaches it for three years and then passes it to us as our co-mission at the end of each of the four gospels. See my book **Christ for the Common Man, chapters 5 and 7**. Christ's mission statement can be summarized as three points:

Christ's Mission —- Our Great Co-Mission Luke 4:18
   1. **Preach the gospel (salvation)**

   2. **Heal (in all its forms)**

   3. **Cast out demons**

Every Christian church in the world preaches the

Great Commission, but we so often stop after salvation is reached. That teaching is for another day. We focus on getting ourselves to heaven and forget the spiritual battle raging in the heavens and on earth. It's a battle to show the ultimate glory and supremacy of God —- and there is no other. We are so self-absorbed we forget about God's calling on our lives; "Just get me to heaven when I die." The three points shown here are to set us **free** so we can join Jesus in His overall mission; here is the overall view from a hundred-thousand feet.

> Little children, let no one deceive you. He who practices righteousness is righteous, just as He is righteous. [8] He who sins is of the devil, for the devil has sinned from the beginning. **For this purpose the Son of God was manifested, that He might destroy the works of the devil.**   1 John 3:7-8

This is the overarching purpose; this is why Jesus was revealed to mankind so we can follow Him and join Him in His mission —- **"that He (Jesus) might destroy the works of the devil."** Notice, Jesus did not come to destroy the devil, but to destroy **the works** of the devil. God will deal with Satan at the end when he and his demons are cast into the lake of fire. Jesus came to destroy Satan's works, his accomplishments and victories; and they are all concentrated in and focused on mankind —- especially the children of God, Christians. That's part of what it means to be set **free** —- free from Satan and sin. The entire New Testament screams of freedom —- **freedom IN CHRIST.**

Christ's invitation to "follow Me" is not an invitation to "come in and take it easy; you just sit in your prayer chair and I will do all the work." You are to pursue healing and wholeness for yourself and then go out into the world setting others free and leading them to Jesus. And you are to join our Master in the battle against His enemy, helping Him to **destroy the works of the devil** bringing freedom and victory to all who are willing to receive it. And you do it all in Jesus' name —- in His divine **authority**.

That's why you are called the **body of Christ**; He is not here, but you are. I don't fully understand the heavenly hosts, but I believe that includes the angels and all those who have left this life for new life in heaven. If you are saved, one day you will be part of the heavenly hosts; the Hebrew word means **armies**.

> [1] In the beginning was the Word, and the Word was with God, and the Word was God. [2] He was in the beginning with God. ... ... vs14 And **the Word became flesh** and dwelt among us, and we beheld His glory, the glory as of the only begotten of the Father, full of grace and truth.   John 1:1-14

It's worth saying again. You are called to be the body —- the living flesh —- of Christ —- right here and now. God still wants this spiritual Word to become a physical Word alive in the flesh on the earth **today** to manifest (reveal, show, demonstrate, make known) the Living God. In answering Christ's call to "follow Me," you are called to **be** and **do** what He was and did. How can that be possible? Christ offers to you the same anointing of power the Father gave to Him —- in the Holy Spirit. But that's for another writing; it is much too big for this little book.

Jesus used His divine authority to deal with demonic attacks, authority given by the Father. He offers this same authority to you.

For discussion and meditation:

Do you want it —- or not???

Will you be part of His army of hosts today —- or not???

Will you be the Word of God in the flesh —- or not???

What would that look like in your life?

Are you sure Jesus is right for you —- or not???

CHAPTER 10

THE STRONG MAN

Remember the big picture of AUTHORITY —- DOMINION ON EARTH.

1. **God gave it to Mankind.**

2. **Mankind gave it to Satan in the garden.**

3. **Jesus comes to take it back.**

4. **The resurrected Jesus offers it again to Mankind by grace through faith.**

In the New Testament writings, Jesus has entered the world; and He refers to Satan as "ruler of this world" John 14:30 and "God of the whole world" 1st John 5:19. Paul refers to Satan as "the god of this age" 2nd Corinthians 4:4.

How can that be? It's because at that time **Satan holds the authority.** Adam and Eve traded it for a piece of fruit. That has to be the world's worst trade.

In the writings of Matthew, Mark, Luke, and John, Jesus has entered the world which is now under **authority** held by Satan; and He has come to **take it back**. "Then one was brought to Him who was **demon-possessed**, blind and mute; and He healed him, so that the blind and mute man both spoke and saw." Matthew 12:22 This man was **possessed/owned/captured** by Satan —- **until Jesus set him free.**

When the Pharisees accused Jesus of exercising Satan's power to cast out demons, He said He could not be of Satan's household using Satan's power against Satan's demons because a house divided against itself must fall.

> Or how can one enter a **strong man's house** and plunder his goods, **unless he first binds the strong man**? And then he will plunder his house. [30] He who is not with Me is against Me, and he who does not gather with Me scatters abroad.   Matthew 12:29-30

He states an important, and seemingly obvious, lesson —- first bind the strong man. But we don't seem to get it. When anything involves demons or the supernatural, the "nice, educated" Christians fall apart. Instead of binding Satan, Christians bury their heads under the covers. It's because of our ignorance; we just will not believe Jesus! If Satan is the god of this world, then **we are in his house**. And just because we're sitting in church, the house of God, that doesn't mean demons aren't sitting right around us. Go back to the previous chapter, and read it again.

^{18} And He said to them, "I saw Satan fall like lightning from heaven. ^{19} **Behold, I give you the authority to trample on serpents and scorpions, and over all the power of the enemy,** and nothing shall by any means hurt you. Luke 10:17-19

I once joined a Sunday School class in a mainline church where the president was a wonderful Spirit-filled man who began each class with a prayer binding the enemy and telling Satan he had no authority and no place in that classroom. At first, that seemed odd —- then comfortable —- then wonderful as I realized I could then teach without any opposition coming from the enemy.

Why don't we begin every Sunday School class and every worship service with such a prayer of binding the enemy of God?

Let's look again at His statement about binding the strong man and see the next verse; I'll bet you miss something important and highly unusual.

Or how can one enter a strong man's house and plunder his goods, unless he first binds the strong man? And then he will plunder his house. ^{30} **He who is not with Me is against Me, and he who does not gather with Me scatters abroad.** Matthew 12:29-30

WOW! If Jesus is our Lord, He actually requires us to be active and **do** something to **demonstrate** it. The comfortable Christian may not be a Christian after all

—- according to the definition Jesus gives.   **OUCH !!!**
If I am not actively **"with"** Jesus, He says I'm **against**
Him. If I am not actively "gathering," Jesus says I'm
scattering.

Christ says there is no comfortable mid-
dle-of-the-road, no place in His kingdom for
pew-warmers. And worst of all, the folks who thought
they were respectable Christians, are **"against Me."**
I've always been nice and respectable, what did I do
wrong??? That's the problem, I did nothing —- nothing
to put my faith into action. The Bible tells us that **"faith**
without works is dead." James 2:14, 2:18, 2:20, 2:26. I
think Jesus is affirming that an inactive dead faith will
not produce eternal life.

Watch this progression:

> And I also say to you that you are Peter, and
> on this rock I will build My church, and the
> gates of Hades shall not prevail against it.
> [19] And I will give you the **keys of the king-**
> **dom of heaven**, and whatever **you bind** on
> earth will be bound in heaven, and whatever
> **you loose** on earth will be loosed in heaven."
> Matthew 16:18-19

Keys represent unlimited **access** and **authority**. Jesus
expects you to **use them**. You bind. You loose.

> "Assuredly, I say to you, whatever **you bind**
> on earth will be bound in heaven, and what-

ever **you loose** on earth will be loosed in heaven.

[19] "Again I say to you that if two of you agree on earth concerning anything that they ask, it will be done for them by My Father in heaven. [20] For where two or three are gathered together in My name, I am there in the midst of them." Matthew 18:18-20

Can you hear His repeated assurances? If only you will have the faith and the courage to act. **Just do it. "If you will, I will."**

God can restrain Satan in your life --- but **He has given that Authority to YOU.**

Lord Jesus died to guarantee that authority in your life —- and **He expects YOU to use it!**

For discussion and meditation:

Why don't we begin every Sunday School class and every worship service with a prayer to bind the enemy of God?

"He who is not with Me is against Me, and he who does not gather with Me scatters abroad." That is tough! Jesus said it, but can it really be true?

This binding and loosing sounds really weird; could it be true? Has anyone I know ever done that?

Why is my church or denomination silent about all this? It is in the Bible!

Does this mean Jesus expects **me** to ever cast out demons?

CHAPTER 11

A MINOR TESTIMONY

I've been so focused on Biblically proving the point, I almost forgot to give you an example. This is important primarily to show you that casting out demons is not some wild and weird process reserved for men in black robes and funny hats. Oh, demons can be wild, and some extreme cases are not for just anyone to handle. There are those who are greatly experienced in such matters; I am not one of them. This is not a game or a contest to show how tough you are. It is part of following Jesus in this tough world. As Jesus was preparing His disciples for His death, He began to let them know they could expect opposition from the world, and in John chapter 17, He prays a beautiful prayer for all believers asking for their protection from **the evil one**. Notice His progression in these verses.

A servant is not greater than his master.' If they persecuted Me, they will also persecute you. John 15:20

In the world you will have tribulation; but be
of good cheer, I have overcome the world."
John 16:33

**I do not pray that You should take them out
of the world, but that You should keep them
from the evil one.** John 17:15

We Christians seem to think the goal of life is to get
out of here and into heaven. Jesus said: "you shall **be**
witnesses unto me" throughout the world. The word
Christian means little Christ, again, the body of Christ.
Peter said: "you are a chosen generation, a royal priesthood." As such, we should expect the same or similar
opposition as our Lord received. Jesus was accosted by
Satan himself from the very beginning of his ministry
when led into the desert. He was accosted by demons
and demonized people on a routine basis throughout
His three-year ministry. But we have been taught to be
so oblivious to this presence that most who will read
this book will not be able to think of a single instance
when the demonic has been present in their lives. That
is not a criticism, and you have no reason to feel foolish.
We simply have not been taught. It's much easier, and
so much nicer, to just ignore the demonic as something
reserved for kooks and people who are "not like us." I
repeat, if you think of demons somewhat as you think
of germs, you will be on the right track. They are present everywhere, and we should be aware —- not afraid,

but aware and able to protect ourselves and loved ones when needed. Wash your hands —- and know how to apply antiseptic when needed.

> [8] Be sober, be vigilant; because your adversary the devil walks about like a roaring lion, seeking whom he may devour. [9] Resist him 1 Peter 5:8-9

> Resist the devil and he will flee from you. James 4:7

To help my teaching, I learned how to use PowerPoint and bought a projector to use with my laptop. It's a terrific teaching aid allowing the visual parts to enhance and improve the audible. The set-up process was simple; you just plug one cable into the laptop and also into the projector; turn it on and everything links together automatically. Even I can handle plug-and-play. One morning as I was setting up in a Sunday School classroom, the projector and the laptop refused to sync. We had about thirty minutes before class time, but I'm not skilled with that. When a young man popped in just to say hello, I grabbed him to help because he was very good with such things. Thirty minutes later as class was beginning, the projector still would not sync and function. The thought came to mind that demons could be involved as the lesson included teaching on dcmons; so I began praying to Jesus to cast them out. It seemed the right thing to do. The Lord spoke to me as clear as a bell. *"Do you really want that?"* Yes, I do; it helps greatly with the teaching, and it's about demons. *"Do you really believe all that about casting out demons?"* Yes, I really do. Then He said as clear as a bell: **"Well, what are you whining to Me for? Do it yourself."** You see, I have that kind of blunt, smart-aleck nature to talk just like that. So, He let me have it full force —- and I just broke down laughing.

Okay —- here's your demonstration. I sat down on the front row with my back to the class, so they wouldn't think I was nuts, and I began to command them to get out. You must speak out loud; they are spirit beings but they cannot read your mind. I just did what Jesus did.

Speak out loud.

Speak calmly.

Speak firmly with total confidence in your God-given authority. This meant I spoke "in Jesus' name and in the authority He has given me." "Behold, I give you the authority to trample on serpents and scorpions, and over all the power of the enemy, and nothing shall by any means hurt you." Luke 10:19

I will sometimes command them "get out" and sometimes "go to Jesus" so He can deal with them.

After thirty minutes of my young friend trying to make it work, I prayed for about ten seconds, and bingo —- the screen lit up with my PowerPoint and everything worked flawlessly. Okay, this little event won't make it into the record books, but that's what I've been telling you. The Bible shows demons to be a commonplace part of life for Jesus and all who will follow Him. Satan is called "the enemy" by Jesus as He offers His authority to us so we might defeat this enemy. If you are a faithful follower, a disciple, of Jesus Christ, then Satan is also your enemy and you are his. You may not "do demons," but the demons want to do you. Peter said Satan prowls around like a roaring lion seeking whom he may devour. That has not changed, and will not change until God casts Satan and his followers into the firey hell prepared for them. Until that time, that's just how it is. If you want the devil to leave you alone, then turn your back on Jesus. So long as you are Christ's friend, you will be Satan's enemy.

This little testimony with the PowerPoint projector is insignificant in my life. There are other stories that you would consider totally insignificant and even silly, though they are true. But then there are stories of spiritual warfare in my life that involved imminent financial ruin for my wife and myself. We were headed for financial ruin, but God allowed me to see His angels standing guard and later see the presence of the enemy's demons. I did what scripture teaches, casting them out, and there followed a twelve-month construction project and reparations that made us whole again. The entire battle lasted for three years. You can read about it in chapter twenty-two of my book, <u>Christ for the Common Man</u>.

For discussion and meditation:

Am I going to believe this?

If casting out can be sometimes a little thing and sometimes a huge, life-changing thing, am I willing to just try it on some little things?

CHAPTER 12

TESTIMONY OF DELIVERANCE AND INNER HEALING

This testimony comes from a personal friend whom I have known and respected for more than twenty years. He chooses to remain anonymous to insure that others, who do not understand spiritual warfare, do not diminish his professional work and his broad-ranging personal ministry.

It was October of 2007, and my knee had received an MRI; the damage had been reviewed by the surgeon, and we were scheduled for surgery in November. So how would I handle work, the holidays, and a busy ministry schedule as I get ready for surgery. Knee damage from an old football injury had to be the reason for this surgery was my thought. The wear and tear of an ex-athlete's life had caught up to me.

The next move was to clear my schedule. I called the friend whom I worked with on a prison ministries team as we were scheduled for the same time as the surgery. He asked if I would stop by his office, and I was only about two minutes away. He met me at the door; the small conference room near the entrance was occupied with people from all over the world. The ten people there came from South America, Africa, various parts of America, and there were several from the Chattanooga area. Once there was a pause in their meeting, I was walked into the room; my friend placed his hand on my shoulder and said, "this is my friend and we need to pray for him." At that point I looked around the room filled with people looking so different from me, and I said, "that is not necessary but I will pray for you." Isn't it strange how we just want to escape an uncomfortable spiritual situation? Instead of welcoming help from the Body of Christ, we just want to escape this strange situation. We're so afraid of the unknown. At that point, a small brown-skinned lady from Trinidad jumped up, pointed right at me, and said "you have a demonic snake wrapped around your knee." Now I knew something strange was going on in my world. How did this stranger know this? And a snake? The next thing I did was say yes to this little lady to receive prayer. All the people gathered around me and anointed my head with oil; they laid hands on me and started praying in languages I had never heard. Speaking in tongues to this United Methodist, traditional downtown church, forty-nine year old man was surely something I had never heard before. And then, for the first time in four months, I went down on my right knee with no pain; I leaned back on that knee with full body weight on the right side and no pain whatsoever. What had just happened? I was not really sure, but I thanked God for this physical healing in my life. For years to come, anytime I would go on my knees I would thank God for the healing and casting out of a demon. About three months later, I had a dream in which the snake was crawling across the wall of my friend's office and I took my shoe off, clubbed it in the head, and killed it. When I awakened from my sleep, I remembered the dream; that is so rare to me. I called my friend and told him of this dream. He told me the lady from Trinidad had just arrived in the U.S. the same evening as when I had the dream. She was actually standing next to my friend when I told him of this vision.

Here is the biggest thing I learned from this really strange experience --- spiritual warfare is real! I no longer had the right to remain ignorant of it, and I needed to learn and claim what God's Word teaches about it in order to protect myself and my family from this kind of evil.

I believe the whole experience stemmed from a crazy work relationship with a man who was my boss for eight years. Oddly enough, he was a leader in his church. Each day it seemed as if I was never performing well enough. Even my most productive days were never good enough; there was only criticism. I had allowed this person to start influencing my thoughts and actions in almost every part of my life. You see, I had been told as a teenager that I would never make it. I was not good enough and never would be. Now, almost fifty years old, I was believing it even though the company had grown from seventy employees to over two-hundred employees and production had more than doubled. I would never be good enough. I was being recognized as a leader in the industry and even presenting classes to international groups on how we had achieved such growth. We had become world leaders in certain new technology in the industry. But every week I heard "we need more; do it now," and the threats and body language toward me were demeaning.

Somehow this stronghold had been established in my work life and in my inner, personal life. I was not good enough. And as if to confirm that, I was now in real physical pain with the knee. That knee was definitely not good enough. But God in His mercy brought together these unique people from distant lands and this strange little lady from Trinidad to take the authority Christ offers us and cast out the agents of the devil --- the one whom Jesus simply calls "the enemy."

That day I received both physical healing for physical pain and inner healing for inner pain. I was truly set free. This stronghold had been put on my body and in my mind by the enemy, until one wonderful day, in ways I never imagined, and by unusual people I had never known, I was SET FREE.

I learned to put on the armor of God, loose the Spirit, bind the enemy, and take responsibility for myself and my family to fight this battle as the devil wants to kill, steal, and destroy, while Christ wants us to live in his abundance. Don't run; stand firm and watch God work as you claim His promises for your life. They are written forever in His Word.

And whatever you do, don't limit God !

CHAPTER 13

HOW DO YOU KNOW?

This is not a how-to-do-demons book. I'm not into that sort of thing, and it certainly is not a game. However, recognizing the presence of evil is always the difficult part. Again, think of germs. Unless you live in a science lab, you've never seen one. And think of illnesses. When you **feel** sick, you go to the doctor; he makes a diagnosis and may write a prescription. His diagnosis may be correct, and his prescription may correct your problem; but it's not always so. Any one of those steps may miss the mark. This sounds very loose, but you know when your life just doesn't feel right. So you may take precautions; you may follow Christ's example of commanding demons to depart. If you are mistaken in your premonition, so what? You appplied the proper treatment or response for an issue that did not exist. No problem —- nothing is lost. If you took a pill prescribed for a physical condition that didn't exist. So what? As with all sensing or feelings, the more experience or practice you have, the more accurate you become. You begin to more readily recognize those times when external factors are obviously going wrong with no rational reason for them.

Chance or accident may explain some things, but there are times when it is clearly more than just a string of "bad luck." And you do know there's no such thing as luck. At times, you have clearly recognized the hand of God in your life as He blesses or protects you. So also you can come to recognize, or sense, the hand of the enemy as he seeks to bring harm. Remember, the Bible tells us that God wants to exalt you, and the devil wants to devour or destroy you —- not just sometimes, but always.

God and Satan have one thing in common — neither one of them takes a day off.

A constant theme throughout this book is the example and teaching of Jesus as He presents Satan and his demons as simply an ongoing and everyday reality to be dealt with. And His prescribed method is to cast them out —- command them to leave. I have quoted Luke 10:17-19 in each of the three previous chapters. You know Jesus has **offered** to you His authority over all the powers of the devil; so **believe it** —- **receive it** —- and **apply it in your daily life**.

Why are you so hesitant; what's the big deal?

For discussion and meditation:

Why am I hesitant? Am I so scared of other people's opinions of me?

Why am I scared of being called a Pentecostal or charismatic? Didn't Jesus start the whole outpouring of power thing at Pentecost?

Will I walk away from this whole spiritual warfare thing just because I'm afraid of other people or afraid I'll make a mistake?

If I do make a mistake somehow, does Holy Spirit still live within me and protect me when I make a mistake?

If this is part of the Great Commission, will I ignore it just because my friends ignore it?

CHAPTER 14

DON'T YOU KNOW WHO YOU ARE?

We tend to view ourselves as weak little people outclassed by the mighty devil, Satan. In truth, he is the powerless one. Go back and read chapter three again. Like the Jews receiving reports of giants from the twelve men sent to spie out the promised land, we see ourselves as insignificant grasshoppers. "There we saw the giants (the descendants of Anak came from the giants); and we were like grasshoppers in our own sight, and so we were in their sight." Numbers 13:33 We are too willing to believe Satan's lies and give in to his bluff of pretended power; we see our physical strength and totally miss the **spiritual strength** Jesus has offered to every believer. With all our worldly education and experience, we are blind to the powers and the battles raging in the spirit realm. How can so many Christians be so ignorant of God's Word?

As Americans, we are accustomed to demanding our rights in every area of life —- except one —- **in Christ.** We have been persuaded —- **by the enemy** —- that demanding those rights would be unfair to others who reject Christ. We should forego those rights in Christ just because others reject Him. And we go along with that so we will not offend anyone; and we dare not offend the new American gods of Diversity, Equity, and Inclusion. As we deny the fullness of Christ, don't you think **we offend God???**

Don't you know who you are if you have accepted Jesus?

Can't you see yourself as God sees you if you have accepted Jesus???

Children of God —- "The Spirit Himself bears witness with our spirit that we are children of God, [17] and if children, then heirs—heirs of God and joint heirs with Christ," Romans 8:16-17

Bride of Christ —- as a metaphor

Ambassadors for Christ —-   "We are ambassadors for Christ" 2 Cor 5:20

Branches in Christ —- "I am the Vine, ye are the branches" John 15:5

Citizens of heaven —- "Fellow citizens with the saints and of the household of God" Eph 2:19

Disciples —- "Whosoever doth not bear his cross, and come after Me, cannot be My disciple" Luke 14:27

Friends —- "Ye are My friends if ye do whatsoever I command you" John 15:14

Heirs —-   "Heirs of God and joint heirs with Christ . . . . that we may be also glorified together" Rom 8:17

Jewels —— "They shall be Mine, saith the Lord of Hosts, in that day when I make up My jewels" Mal 3:17

Kings and Priests —- "Made us kings and priests unto God and His Father" Revelation 1:6

Light of the world —- "You are the light of the world.

Let your light so shine," Matt 5:14

Members of Christ's body —- "For we are members of His body" Eph 5:30

New Creatures in Christ —- "If any man be in Christ he is a new creature" 2Cor 5:17

Redeemed ones —- "You were not redeemed with corruptible things.....but with the precious blood of Christ" 1 Peter 1:18

Temple of God —- "Know you not that you are the temple of God, and that the Spirit of God dwells in you?" 1 Cor 3:16

WOW — that sounds like an important and impressive bunch of people to me — surely not grasshoppers!

If you think it's possible that God sees you correctly —- then believe Him —- trust His judgment.

Be the person God believes you are.

Try it; it may be scary at first, but just try it. You won't be alone; the One who said "I will never leave you nor forsake you will stand beside you." Jesus will stand with you against the devil and all his demons. I promise you; He makes good His promises. If you can trust Him for eternity, why can't you trust Him for today? **Just try it —- and you will find out who the real grasshoppers are.**

"For this purpose the Son of God was manifested, that He might destroy the works of the devil." 1 John 3:8

For discussion and meditation:

How do I see yourself —- as a Grasshopper or Child of God ?

Think through each of the listed titles for yourself in scripture; what do you look like in that role?

Can you begin to see yourself in that role and actually live like you are that person?

What will it take for you to **be** the person God believes you **are**?

CHAPTER 15

YOU CAN DO THIS !

Dear friend, I've tried to show you who you are in Christ —- if you have accepted Him as your savior. You are not some helpless little grasshopper. You belong to God. You are the beloved bride of Jesus Christ. The Spirit of God lives within you as God's seal. This is not some generic description for an entire class of beings; this is God's description of **you** (insert your name here) individually.

Here I will close with God's principles, for He is wonderfully consistent.

All of God's offers of blessing come by Grace through Faith —- God's hand of grace touching your hand of faith.

1. **You Believe it by Faith**

2. **You Receive it by Faith**

3. **You Live it by Faith.**

From the beginning, God's offers of blessing have always involved an obligation for us to obey His laws.

As New Testament Christians, saved by grace through faith, we too easily forget God's call to obedience. Grace is so much more appealing; freebies are always good. But since the beginning of man, God has called us to obey; and with that call comes a promise of reward if we do and loss of rewards if we don't. I find it's good to go back to the beginning in trying to understand God. After all, In the last book of the Old Testament, He says "I am the Lord God; I do not change." Malachi 3:6 And Jesus said He came to fulfill the Old Testament law, not destroy or replace it. Consider these teachings as Moses taught the words and ways of God to the people of God.

> Now, O Israel, listen to the statutes and the judgments which I teach you to **observe** [**do, obey**], that you may live, and go in and possess the land which the Lord God of your fathers is giving you.   Deuteronomy 4:1

> Now it shall come to pass, if you diligently **obey** the voice of the Lord your God, to **observe** [**do, obey**] carefully all His commandments which I command you today, that the Lord your God will set you high above all nations of the earth. [2] And all these blessings shall come upon you and overtake you, because you **obey** the voice of the LORD your God: Deuteronomy 28:1-2

When God put on flesh and came to earth to live among us, He had to learn to obey as part of His humanity.

> Though He [Jesus] was a Son [of God], yet
> **He learned obedience** by the things which
> He suffered. Hebrews 5:8

Obedience is part of the Great Commission as given in Matthew's gospel.

> Go therefore and make disciples of all the
> nations, baptizing them in the name of the
> Father and of the Son and of the Holy Spirit,
> 20 teaching them to **observe [do, obey]** all
> things that I have commanded you; and lo, I
> am with you always, even to the end of the
> age." Matthew 28:19-20

You verify your Faith by your actions —- your works —- the life you live.
Jesus is all about life —- abundant and eternal. This little book is not about theology or some theory —- it's about life —- a life of Victory in Christ. We don't have His victory if we are not living daily in Him. Jesus is the Way, Truth, and Life —- we are to live and walk in His Way, Truth, and Life. None of this is academic; it is the ultimate reality; it is the life you live. **Your actions, reveal and verify your salvation and new life in Christ.**

> But do you want to know, O foolish man,
> that faith without **works** is dead? 21 Was not

Abraham our father justified by **works** when he offered Isaac his son on the altar? [22] Do you see that faith was working together with his **works**, and by **works** faith was made perfect? [23] And the Scripture was fulfilled which says, "Abraham believed God, and it was accounted to him for righteousness." And he was called the friend of God. [24] You see then that a man is justified by **works**, and not by faith only. James 2:20-24   See also: James 2:14, 18, 20, 26

Spiritual warfare is real today —- and you are in it if you are in Christ. But never fear for you will never be alone. Hear Paul's benediction.

"The grace of the Lord **Jesus Christ**, and the love of **God**, and the communion (constant and complete union) of the **Holy Spirit** be with you all. Amen" 2 Corinthians 13:14

You have the assurance of God's love, brought to you in grace by Jesus. You have the constant **presence** of God because His Spirit lives within you. And you have the **power** of God through His Spirit. And all of this is right there living in your tee shirt. God the Father, Son, and Spirit are all longing for a deeply personal and constant relationship with you.

What more could you need or ask?

You can do this.

For discussion and meditation:

Obedience just doesn't sound like fun. Why is it so hard to look beyond the obligation and see the rewards it will bring?

Could the call to obedience be Christ's constant reminder of who we are in Him?

Is the call to obedience also a call to consistency —- to remembering who I am in Christ?

CHAPTER 16

JESUS WON; NOW IT'S ON YOU.

He has won the victory, now we must live it out in our lives.
We are to establish His kingdom here on earth making His truth to become our reality.

> And Jesus came and spoke to them, saying, "All authority has been given to Me in heaven and on earth. Go therefore and make disciples of all the nations, baptizing them in the name of the Father and of the Son and of the Holy Spirit, teaching them to observe [to do, fulfill, complete] all things that I have commanded you; and lo, I am with you always, even to the end of the age." Matthew 28:18-20

Lord Jesus declared victory —- His victory over sin and Satan —- and then bowed His head and surrendered his spirit as man, ready to go home to His heavenly home.

The battle is over and the victory is won; Christ has
gone home —- but someone has to establish His victory
on earth. Someone has to establish His kingdom as
reality here on earth. No leader wins a territory and
then abandons it to be retaken by the enemy. The Body
of Christ, the church, is charged with that task. We are
to be the physical presence of Jesus here and now. We
are to bring the spiritual Kingdom of God to reality in
this physical world. Each one of the four gospels ends
with Christ passing the baton of His mission —- and
His victory — to us. We call it the Great Commission.

At the end of And Jesus came and spoke to them,
saying, "All authority has been given to Me in heaven
and on earth. Go therefore and make disciples of all
the nations, baptizing them in the name of the Father
and of the Son and of the Holy Spirit, teaching them to
observe [to do, fulfill, complete] all things that I have
commanded you; and lo, I am with you always, even to
the end of the age."   Matthew 28:18-20

It is called spiritual warfare for a good reason. But no
war was ever won and no peace ever established by a
defensive life.

So when Jesus had received the sour
wine, He said, "It is finished!" And bowing His head, He gave up His spirit.
John 19:30

After World War 1, France wanted to insure their fu-
ture safety from attack by Germany; heavy debate fol-

lowed as how best to do that. General Charles de Gaulle
wanted to develop an offensive force based on speed,
mobility, and mechanized vehicles. But others were
afraid of offending Germany, even though **the war was
over and the victory won**. So France built a continuous
line of defensive fortifications along the entire border
with Germany; it was known as the Maginot line. **Afraid
of offending a known and dangerous enemy, they
chose a policy consisting only of defense.** Less than
twenty-five years later, German forces simply bypassed
the Maginot fortifications with their tanks —- "speed,
mobility, and mechanized vehicles" —- and occupied
Paris.

Does this sound like anything today as so much of the
church remains silent in the face of Satan's attack using
all manner of woke ideologies and diluted versions of
God's Word.

**"If we speak out against it, we will offend others."
Tolerance** is our preferred response, and churches
wrestle today with how far they should go with em-
bracing new moralities and replacing old theologies.
The church has been handed Christ's victory bought
with His precious blood, and yet we are afraid we will
offend if we speak in strength to enforce His victory and
fulfill our commission of "teaching them to observe [to
do, fulfill, complete] all things that I have commanded
you." Love and kindness are at the heart of the gospel
of Jesus. Tolerance isn't mentioned.

The first biblical mention of the church:
Jesus answered and said to him, "I will build my
church." Just notice our language as we speak of "my
church" and "our church" and plan ways we will build

our church. Jesus said it is His church and He will build it. He said our job is you shall be witnesses unto me. We are to do that by living out His victory in our lives and demonstrating the power available to all who will enter into His kingdom here and now.

"The gates of Hades shall not prevail against it." The Greek for prevail means to have superior strength or power. Gates are defensive, to defend hell and its occupants —- to defend Satan and his demons from Jesus and His saints. **Hell should be the one on defense.** Jesus sees His church as being on the offense; why do we see it as being on the defense? Jesus tells us to **go;** why do we remain so passive and want to **stay** inside the church walls?

But YOU must act on it; YOU are the CHURCH.
Jesus says if YOU will act, HE will respond.
The Son of God has done all of this for you —- and offered all this to you —- what will you do with His offer?
Wake up Church!
There is no automatic door opener; you have to use your keys.
It's time to BE the Church.
Let's put on our boots.

Jesus fought the battle and won the victory; He hands it to you.
Will you have the courage to accept it?
He offers a "Commission" in His army.
Will you accept it?

For discussion and meditation:

This is beginning to sound like work and obligation; do I really have to do anything?

I thought Christianity was all about getting freebies: eternal life, blessings, and good stuff.

Just because Jesus paid the price for my sins, and paid with His own blood, do I really have any obligation to Him?

Is my natural, human tendency selfishness? It's all about me; isn't it?

I love Jesus as my Savior, but what does "Lord" really mean?

CHAPTER 17

DOWN-AND-OUT, OR UP-AND-OUT

It's all the same; both are just OUT.

Many Christians live lives of constant mediocrity —- without ever experiencing great defeat or victory. They are never very evil nor very great; they're just "nice" —- and eventually numb. The pain is never great enough to cry out to God. The danger is never great enough to feel the need of God. Life is just "okay." The sad irony in this is that they miss so much of the joy of overcoming, the victory and blessing Jesus wants to give. They miss it simply because they are too blind to see their lives as Jesus sees. Some never cry out because they are too numb to feel or too blind to see. And some never cry out because they just don't believe He will answer. God's love, Christ's sacrifice, Holy Spirit's constant presence —- it's simply wasted on them —- because some cannot believe it's true and will not receive.

A dear friend of mine has an unbelievable ministry

through Celebrate Recovery. As an evangelist and mu-
sician, he works primarily with those struggling with
the various addictions and difficulties of life, and boy
do they respond to him. If you've never battled a major
life-controlling addiction, you may view these folks as
down and out. But Jesus holds a special love for them,
and their struggles can be a real source of blessing. He
loves to heal broken lives and restore them to wholeness — if only they will ask. Christ loves to grab the
down and out and bring them up and in —- into His
kingdom.

> Blessed are those who hunger and thirst
> for righteousness, for they shall be filled.
> Matthew 5:6

> And Jesus said to them, "I am the bread of
> life. He who comes to Me shall never hunger,
> and he who believes in Me shall never thirst.
> John 6:35

The down and out understand their circumstance,
and they hunger and thirst for deliverance.

The up and out are simply comfortable; they are
"okay" and numb to their need.

The church today is filled with such folks; they are like
the church at Laodecia. They thought they were on top
of the world with no struggles and no needs they could
not handle. They thought they were hot stuff, but they
were merely lukewarm and just kidding themselves.
Jesus tells how He sees them.

"I know your works, that you are neither cold nor hot. I could wish you were cold or hot. [16] So then, because you are lukewarm, and neither cold nor hot, I will vomit you out of My mouth. [17] Because you say, I am rich, have become wealthy, and have need of nothing'—and do not know that you are wretched, miserable, poor, blind, and naked— [18] I counsel you to buy from Me gold refined in the fire, that you may be rich; and white garments, that you may be clothed, that the shame of your nakedness may not be revealed; and anoint your eyes with eye salve, that you may see. [19] As many as I love, I rebuke and chasten. Revelation 3:15-19

They had plenty of the world's gold but none of His. They had fine clothes and high fashion but none of His robes of righteousness. He describes them as blind to the truth, and He longs to anoint their eyes so they may see the light of His Truth.

The down-and-out hunger and thirst for righteousness —- **for more of Jesus. He said they shall be filled.**

The up and out are comfortable and satisfied within themselves. They just think they're full.

How are you today, my friend? Whether you are up or down, I pray you're not comfortable, satisfied, or lukewarm. Jesus said, "So then, because you are lukewarm, and neither cold nor hot, I will vomit you out of My mouth." Jesus longs to bless those who hunger and thirst.

You don't get to choose the circumstances of your birth and childhood nor of life itself, but you do choose your response. And most important of all, you choose which of the two great spiritual powers will influence your life. You get to choose whom you will believe and follow.

> *Therefore humble yourselves under the mighty hand of God, that **He MAY exalt** you in due time, [7] casting all your care upon Him, for He cares for you. [8] Be sober, be vigilant; because your adversary the devil walks about like a roaring lion, seeking whom **he MAY devour**. [9] **Resist** him, steadfast in the **faith**, knowing that the same sufferings are experienced by your brotherhood in the world. 1 Peter 5:6-*

Dear friends, the world's definition of success has always been false. All the money in the world will never be enough to buy the fruit of God's Spirit. **"But the fruit of the Spirit is love, joy, peace, longsuffering, kindness, goodness, faithfulness, gentleness, and self-control."** Galatians 5:22-23

The down-and-out and the up-and-out have one big thing in common —- they're both out.

God wants to exalt you. Satan wants to devour you.
BOTH REQUIRE YOUR PERMISSION.
You choose!

For discussion and meditation:

We're back to that word, "may." So I have this ultimate freedom to choose between God and Satan —- good and evil.

Could this mean that every choice I face is between the good or evil side?

If I go to church every Sunday, why can't I just live my life on my own Monday through Saturday?

Is my entire life supposed to be dedicated to Jesus? Living with Him and for Him? Is that what is meant by the Kingdom of God?

Can the things of this world ever satisfy me?

Is my life really full today —- or running on empty?

CHAPTER 18

BELIEVE THE WORDS OF JESUS.
BELIEVE HIM.

I will close out this little book with the words of Jesus as He teaches us how to pray. It is obviously the best known and most frequently repeated prayer in the history of the world —- the Lord's Prayer. He begins by praising God and worshipping Him and then shifts to petitions for certain things. Remember, this prayer is intended for everyone who worships God; it is not designed for the specific needs of a few or for specific times in our lives. It's a daily prayer for every man. And notice that Jesus did not give this as His perfect prayer to be memorized and recited regularly. He gave it as the **pattern** for our praying. "**In this manner, therefore, pray...** ." Matthew 6:9 This is to be the pattern for all our prayers. Look closely at the next to last line as His final request before closing with additional worship and praise.

And do not lead us into temptation, but DELIVER US from the evil one. Matthew 6:13

"Deliver" means to set free from captivity or persecution, both in English and in Greek. And this is **Christ's petition for everyone.** You cannot be delivered unless there is something or someone from whom to be delivered. You cannot receive deliverance unless you actually need it. And Jesus tells us to pray to God our Father for deliverance from Satan, the evil one. Some translations say from evil, but the word more correctly means evil in person —- Satan. This means Jesus sees every one of us as being under constant attack or persecution from Satan and his demons. Some days are just worse than others. Whether you view it as possessed, oppressed, or depressed, scripture does not bother with such details of degree; Jesus just wants us to be set free —- totally free —- from Satan's constant attack. And He gave this as the pattern for our ordinary, everyday prayers.

You probably never looked at your life as needing deliverance from the demonic. Jesus sees it as an everyday need.

Satan never quits. Think about it; he lost the battle in heaven and was kicked out. He didn't quit. He came to God's perfect earth and won a victory of sorts in the garden; God then put a curse on Satan. But he never quit. He put Jesus to death —- Jesus wouldn't stay dead —- and still Satan never quits.

> So the Lord God said to the serpent: "Be-
> cause you have done this, you are cursed
> more than all cattle, and more than every
> beast of the field; on your belly you shall go,
> and you shall eat dust all the days of your
> life. And I will put enmity [hostility, oppo-
> sition] between you and the woman, and
> between your seed and her Seed [Jesus]; He
> shall bruise your head, and you shall bruise
> His heel." Genesis 3:14-15

There is God's earthly curse and eternal prophecy
for the devil, but **look carefully at how God plans to
fulfill His prophecy.** Look as Paul writes to the Roman
Christians.

> Therefore I am glad on your behalf; but I
> want you to be wise in what is good, and sim-
> ple concerning **evil.** [20] And the **God of peace**
> will crush Satan **under YOUR feet** shortly.
> Romans 16:19-20

GOD makes it happen; it is by His will, authority, and
power. And this refers to the entire Holy Trinity. God
of peace —- Jesus the prince of peace —- Holy Spirit
in whom we find peace (Romans 14:17.) And God uses
you; He expects you to take part in this spiritual battle
to establish His kingdom on earth.

You are God's steward —- boots on the ground.

YOU are God's representative, His steward, a holy priesthood, the living body of Christ —- **boots on the ground** —- **right here and right now** —- "this day." "And God will crush Satan under YOUR feet" —- under your boots. You will experience victory over Satan here and now, in this life —- IN CHRIST. Romans 16:20

Now that is exciting!!! If that won't light your fire, your wood is wet.

And still, the enemy never quits. No matter how badly he is defeated —- he will be back tomorrow. Satan knows full well his eternal destiny is the lake of fire prepared especially for him and his demons "and they will be tormented day and night forever and ever." Revelation 20:10 Imagine that; he has been defeated time and again —- he knows his destiny is final defeat —- but he keeps on attacking the children of God and finds pleasure in each temporary victory he can achieve over your life or mine. It's hard to imagine the hatred and darkness that could drive a creature like that, but that is just who he is.

It is very real. It is real life in what we call the real world.   And it is **daily.** Hear the comprehensive Word of God.

JESUS has a role to play in God's plan:

> **For this purpose the Son of God was manifested, that HE might destroy the works of the devil.** 1 John 3.8

YOU have a role to play in God's plan:

> I give YOU the authority to trample on ser-
> pents and scorpions, and over all the power
> of the enemy. Luke 10:19

YOU must accept Christ's offer and be willing to
wield His authority as a weapon for victory.

> And the God of peace will crush Satan under
> YOUR feet. Romans 16:20

GOD provides the power to do it; YOU provide the
hands and feet.

Praise God the Father, Son, and Spirit!
Praise God for the eternal victory already won.
Praise God for the daily victory that is ours in Christ
and His authority.
Praise God for a faithful promise: "I will never leave
you nor forsake you."
PRAISE GOD !!!
AMEN

For discussion and meditation:

What if I just refuse ? ? ?
What if I don't want Christ's Great Comission —-
Co-mission ? ? ?

What if I refuse to serve —- to be God's boots on this ground ? ? ?

What if I just want to be left alone, and I will take care of ME ? ? ?

Think about it !

My weekly blog, "Think about It,"

is available FREE of charge at

www.tompatrick.org

About the Author

Tom Patrick (1941 -) is a native resident of Chattanooga, Tennessee. He earned degrees from Vanderbilt University and Emory University but will quickly tell you his best education came from work experience and from service in the U.S. Army. When President Kennedy was assassinated, Tom was a twenty-one year old tank platoon leader in West Germany at the height of the cold war. What would Russia do? His five tanks would be facing twenty-five Russian tanks. Life was serious; it always has been.

He began working summers loading trucks in a warehouse at the age of eleven, and at sixteen he became a distance truck driver. The laws were less strict then. At nineteen, he went to the oil fields of Oklahoma to work as a roughneck on a drilling rig. There was an accident, and he was crushed by a 1,500 pound drill casing. It took thirty hours to reach a hospital for surgery and followed by a month in bed with morphine injections every four hours and more surgery the next year. It was then he realized that God had intervened to spare his life and surely God had some purpose for that. This was to be the beginning of sixty plus years of miraculous blessings

After military service and graduate school, he joined the family business which was a group of "five and dime" stores. When laws were changed and stores were allowed to open on Sunday, Tom remembered God's deliverance on the oil rig and promised Him that he would never open on Sundays. "I'll shut it down first." Sunday quickly became the second best business day of the week. So in 1982, he began a two year process of liquidating the fifty year old company. He started another retail business which continued until 1997 when he liquidated once again and joined a small-group ministry to businessmen. He would later form his own ministry.

Tom has been teaching in Sunday School and small groups since 1980. Teaching the Bible is his great love and greatest gift. In 1980 he met Pastor Tommy Tyson, a Spirit-filled Methodist evangelist whom he describes as "the most Christlike man I have ever known." Tommy became his mentor and best friend. Here Tom found his source of growth in the Father, the Son, and the Spirit.

Though greatly blessed, life has had its struggles. During the business years, with multiple store locations, he experienced five major fires, two floods, and one sinkhole.

His personal hobbies have included, sailplane pilot, aircraft pilot, motorcycles, boats, tractors, excavators, and serving as volunteer firefighter from age sixty-three to seventy.

Since age 70, a stroke, open heart surgery, and other events have slowed the pace, but life remains full.

Always a member of mainline denominational

churches, his greatest burden and grieving is for Christians who are genuine believers but cannot bring themselves to accept the mystery and miracles in God's supernatural presence by His Holy Spirit. So they settle for life in their own power and accept whatever happens as the will of God, or just bad luck. It is Tom's prayer that this little book will open hearts and minds so that more may know and celebrate the Kingdom of God, the Kingdom of Heaven right here and now —- while on the way to heaven.

Author's Website: www.TomPatrick.org

**A weekly blog is available free of charge at :
www.TomPatrick.org**

Made in the USA
Columbia, SC
13 September 2023

22813618R00064